Original title:

Snowfall and Shimmering Stars

Author: Julian Prescott

ISBN HARDBACK: 978-9916-94-572-8

ISBN PAPERBACK: 978-9916-94-573-5

A Celestial Tapestry of Light and Ice

In the chill of a frosty night,
Snowflakes dance in pure delight.
With mittens lost and noses red,
I trip on ice like a clumsy sled.

The stars above start to giggle,
As I do a funny little wiggle.
Hats fly off in a snowy breeze,
While thumping on my knees, oh please!

Laughter echoes in the dark,
As tow-headed kids ignite a spark.
They throw snowballs that fly like darts,
Missing their targets, aiming for hearts.

Under the glow of shimmering light,
Frosty smiles are quite a sight.
With every slip and silly fall,
Winter wonderland delights us all.

Glacial Serenade Under Twinkling Skies

Stars winking down on snowy peaks,
A chorus of giggles from frosty cheeks.
Tripping over snowmen's hats,
Trying to dance like a bunch of cats.

Puffy coats and frozen toes,
It's all fun 'til someone blows.
A snowball fight ignites with glee,
But I get nailed behind a tree!

The sky is clear and full of gleam,
As laughter flows like a bubbling stream.
In a world where whimsy rules the night,
Even the owls take a break for flight.

So let's cheer for the chilly spree,
With hot cocoa for you and me.
For in the land of sparkling ice,
Each silly moment rolls like dice!

The Frosty Caress of Cosmic Light

In the hush of midnight's chill,
A snowman dances, quite the thrill.
His carrot nose twitches fast,
He sneezes loudly—oh, what a blast!

Under twinkling gems up high,
A penguin slides with a joyous cry.
He turns, he tumbles, oh what a sight,
Waving at the moon—what a delight!

Flickering Echoes in the Quietness

The chilly breeze is up to tricks,
It tickles noses, makes them flick.
A polar bear with ice cream cone,
Chasing his friend on a frosty throne!

With puffy cheeks and icy toes,
An elf gets stuck in a drift—oh no!
But laughter rings, it fills the air,
As they dig him out with tender care!

Chills of Enchantment Overhead

A rabbit hops with fluffy flair,
Wearing goggles—a stylish pair.
He glides on ice, a magical scene,
While squirrels cheer and wave their green!

As winter's breath casts frosty sighs,
The stars are grinning in the skies.
An owl hoots in a joyful tune,
Making the snowflakes dance like a swoon!

An Oasis of Cold Light and Dreams

In the land where the chilly giggles reign,
A mouse spins round on a candy cane.
With marshmallow hats and twinkly shoes,
He sings to the stars, he's got the moves!

Through shimmering air, a comet zips by,
A snowflake's giggle makes the heavens sigh.
As they swirl and twirl, it's quite absurd,
Winter's own ballet, have you heard?

Silent Nights Dressed in Radiance

In a cozy nook, I sip hot chai,
Outside, the flakes swirl, oh my, oh my!
The cat looks puzzled, tail in a twist,
Wondering where all the white stuff's missed.

Bouncing snowmen with carrots in hand,
Wobbling boots can't quite understand.
The snowballs fly, a giggle-filled fight,
As the neighbors shout, 'It's a wild winter night!'

The Frosted Mirror of Heaven's Light

Bright orbs twinkle, like winks in the dark,
Fairy lights blink, and dogs start to bark.
Sleds zoom by on the glistening ground,
As laughter and howls of pure joy abound.

A snow angel's made, with flair and with grace,
But wait! What's this? A plop on my face!
A rogue snowball caught me quite off guard,
With snowflakes in my hair, I feel like a bard!

Twilight Serenade with Dancing Glow

A flurry of glitter, it twinkles and shines,
As I step out, I hear chime-like designs.
The moon wears a crown, the jokes deeply flow,
While squirrels throw acorns, their winter-time show.

And while I sipped cider, oh what a blunder!
I slipped on the ice, turned into a thunder!
Yet laughter erupted, as friends held me tight,
Rolling in snow, feeling pure delight!

Glittering Echoes Across Still Waters

Winter whispers sweetly, as lakes start to freeze,
Ice-skating penguins waddle with ease.
A game of charades with my clumsy friends,
We tumble and giggle, the laughter never ends.

The moon, now a beacon, with shadows that dance,
Spinning in circles, we jump at the chance.
With each playful slip, a memory grows,
As the silver scene twinkles, our joy just flows!

Celestial Mysteries in the Icy Air

Wonders fall from skies so wide,
With frosty flakes that serve as slides.
While kites chase comets in the breeze,
And penguins skate with utmost ease.

Snowmen giggle, hats askew,
With carrot noses asking, 'Who?'
They dance with squirrels on a lark,
While rabbits hop until it's dark.

Glacial Glimmers in the Infinite

Little stars blink in the night,
While snowflakes turn wrongs to right.
A jingle bell on a cat's tail,
Makes winter nights a grand old tale.

Frosty air and hot cocoa cheer,
As snowmen argue, 'I should steer!'
With skiing rabbits, quick as a flash,
They tumble down in a jolly crash.

Trail of Light Beneath the Frozen Canopy

Bright-eyed critters toss snowballs,
With laughter echoing through the halls.
The moon is grinning, fully round,
As snowy mischief shakes the ground.

Icicle chandeliers dangle low,
While frosty whispers gently flow.
With foxes plotting secret schemes,
They dance in silver-threaded dreams.

A Symphony of Stars in Winter's Clutch

A symphony of giggles rise,
As twinkling lights adorn the skies.
The trees all wear their icy crowns,
While snowy caps bring smiles, not frowns.

A bob sled crash and a hearty cheer,
As friends laugh loud, no room for fear.
The stars all wink, as if they know,
Winter's tricks in the frosty glow.

Celestial Veil Over Silent Streets

A blanket of white on the roads so slick,
Even penguins here might do a dance or a trick.
Neighbors slip past with laughter galore,
Their snowballs turn into friendship and more.

The cars look like cupcakes all frosted and sweet,
While squirrels are strutting on tiny frostbitten feet.
Children in layers make snowman with flair,
But watch out for snowballs launched mid-air!

Glimmering Chill Beneath the Cosmos

Stars wink like eyes, all shiny and bright,
While snowflakes land soft, like pillows of white.
A chubby raccoon wears a snow hat so grand,
He glides on the ice like he's head of a band.

The moon beams down with a sassy old wink,
Making snowmen blush and causing them to think.
It's a party tonight, in nature's own way,
Just watch where you're stepping—hippopotamus play!

Frost-Kissed Dreams in Silver Light

A tiny elf sneezes, his hat takes a flight,
It lands on a snowman, what a curious sight!
He chuckles and shakes, stirring flurries of glee,
As snowflakes join forces for zany esprit.

Hot cocoa's afoot, with marshmallows dancing,
While bunnies in mittens keep quietly prancing.
Each sip brings a giggle, oh what a delight,
In a world where the odd is simply just right!

Hushed Sparkles Under the Moon

The moon plays peek-a-boo, hiding away,
While shadows sneak out to join in the play.
A snow angel flops, like a pillow fight,
Who knew frosty fun could feel so light?

Snowflakes are soft as they tickle our cheeks,
Ticklish laughter is what everyone seeks.
With frozen eyebrows and noses like gnomes,
We'll stay up too late, under twinkling homes.

Frozen Echoes and Stellar Currents

Tiny flakes take flight in the night,
They dance around, what a funny sight!
A snowman sneezes, what a big fuss,
With carrot nose, he rides on a bus!

Stars giggle softly, twinkling bright,
They point at snowmen, oh what a sight!
As laughter echoes through the chill,
Ice cream cones launch for a winter thrill!

Nightfall's Caress on Crystal Terrain

Under the moon, snowflakes slide,
Sledding penguins take a wild ride!
A polar bear in a funny spree,
Tries to catch stars while on a spree!

The frosty ground is quite the stage,
With ice capades from a furry sage!
Chasing shadows, round and round,
Everyone's giggling, joy unbound!

Radiance Hidden in Winter's Breath

In the frosty air, chuckles are made,
As snowflakes tickle features, not afraid!
A jolly snowball flies through the night,
Bounces off cheeks, what a delight!

Lights twinkle bright, like a playful game,
Winter's a jokester, never the same!
Snowmen debate on who's more grand,
While shovels dance like a rock band!

Luminous Ribbons on a Crystal Canvas

Glittering trails on the ground below,
A dance party starts with a furry show!
Bunnies in scarves are doing the twist,
In a winter wonder, who'd dare resist?

The night holds secrets, slick and bright,
As creatures conspire for some snowball fight!
With giggles that fill the chilly air,
Bright stars watch closely, a cosmic affair!

The Tapestry of Night and Chill

When the cold decides to throw a dance,
Everyone slips, oh what a chance!
With each flake, a giggle spills,
As we tumble down the frosty hills.

The moon giggles in its silver hue,
While we build forts, yes, that's our cue!
Snowmen sport a carrot nose, quite grand,
We argue over who has the best hand.

Chilly winds hum a playful tune,
While sweaters stretch, oh how they swoon!
We're like penguins, bouncing around,
In the frosty fun that knows no bound.

But when it's time for cocoa warm,
We take a break from the winter charm.
With marshmallows floating, we toast with mirth,
What a wacky show, this winter's birth!

Celestial Gleams on Powdered Earth

Under a quilt of sparkly white,
We trip over glee, what a sight!
With jeweled flakes that dance in air,
We start a snowball fight without a care.

Sleds zoom by, laughter fills the street,
With hot cocoa ready, oh what a treat!
Frosty fingers and cheeks all red,
We make angels, silly, in our bed.

The stars are winking, twinkling bright,
While we chase shadows in that night.
Each gust of wind brings a silly cheer,
To this wintry world we hold so dear.

As the world goes quiet under the glow,
We wrap up warm, and enjoy the show.
We giggle and laugh until the day's spun,
For what's more fun than winter run?

Starry Veil over Frozen Horizons

When the world wears a coat of white,
We grab our sleds, ready for flight!
Down the hills, we zoom with glee,
Laughing like children, wild and free.

Frosty eyebrows and noses bright,
Playful snowflakes whirl, what a sight!
In this winter wonder, we start to slide,
Like penguins waddling, we're full of pride.

The night sky sparkles like a fairy tale,
While we sip on cocoa, hearts set to sail.
With giggles echoing through the trees,
We dare the frost to bring us to our knees.

Beneath the stars, it's sheer delight,
As we play until the morning light.
With that silly grin, we chase the moon,
In this whimsical world, we're over the moon!

A Kaleidoscope of Ice and Light

The ground is a canvas, painted so bright,
We dive into snow, oh what a sight!
Frosted friends with goofy grins,
Twirling around, where the laughter begins.

In fluffy boots, we stomp and prance,
Taking our chances in a twisted dance.
Who knew that icy fun could be,
A whirlwind of giggles and pure glee?

Frozen noses and cheeky pouts,
Explore the landscape, shrieks and shouts!
Our breath is a cloud in the chilly air,
Snowflakes kissing our tousled hair.

So, grab your hat, put on your gloves,
In this icy world, let's all share love.
With the light of the moon shining so bright,
We'll revel in laughter, all through the night!

Twinkling Jewels on a Slope of Silence

Laughter echoes through the night,
A snowball flies with all its might.
Fluffy hats and puffy coats,
We're like penguins, and that's no joke!

Giggling at our frozen toes,
Honey, it's not frostbite, it's just perfume, who knows?
Sledding down the slope with glee,
We might just win the best-ski trophy!

Ethereal Frost Beyond the Horizon

There's someone stuck in a snowdrift,
Sipping cocoa, their whole vibe's a gift.
With marshmallows dancing on their nose,
Is it winter or just a frozen pose?

A squirrel wearing a tiny hat,
Clearly plotting his next snack attack.
We laugh at the antics of the night,
Who knew cold could feel so right?

A Blanket of Light Among the Pines

Trees are wearing frost like it's chic,
While giggly friends play hide-and-seek.
One slips and lands with a silly plop,
Is that a cheer or a scream? Who knows, stop!

Snowflakes pirouette on the breeze,
Like nature's dancers, aiming to tease.
We throw up our arms, catch the drift,
Nature grants us the best comic gift!

Chasing Moonbeams in Celestial Drapes

Under the glow, we dance around,
Staffed with giggles, our joy knows no bounds.
We chase the light, we twirl with glee,
Wishing the stars could come join our spree.

Footprints lead to a marshmallow treat,
But oops! It's gone, swept away on our feet.
With laughter echoing high and bright,
Who knew the stars could sparkle with delight?

An Illumined Path Through a Winter Dream

As flakes parade and dance with glee,
The ground is a stage for a wild jubilee.
A snowman wobbles, top hat askew,
"Oh dear!" he shouts, "I need a new view!"

Mittens join hands in a chilly embrace,
Sleds racing down—what a comical chase!
A puppy dives headfirst in a snowbank,
Emerging with a look that says, "What the—?"

Bright lights twinkle from every tree,
Icicles dangle—truly a sight to see!
A gingerbread man's hat flies like a kite,
"Why is winter so full of delight?"

Laughter erupts, in the frosty air,
With every slip and every wild scare.
A snowball flies—oops! That was me!
We tumble together, happy as can be.

Echoes of Enchantment in the Cold

The chill in the air bites like a tease,
As frost nips noses, but brings us to knees.
Snow angels flapping, what a clumsy sight,
"I swear I'm graceful!"—but not tonight!

A yeti grins from the edge of a hill,
With marshmallows stacked for a sweet winter thrill.
Our hot cocoa spills in a giggling spree,
"More for the snowmen!"—they seem so thirsty!

On frozen ponds, we glide and twirl,
With socks that spark laughter, what a whirl!
"Look at me, Mom!" as I crash in a heap,
"Will I get extra cookies for this goofy sweep?"

Stars wink in the dark, they chuckle with flair,
While we sip on joy, without a single care.
The night's full of magic, as we laugh and cheer,
Creating our legends, all winter long here.

The Mystical Glow in the Frozen Night

Under a blanket, the world starts to play,
Frosty whispers come out to sway.
A penguin waddles, the prince of the scene,
"Who ordered fish frys? I'm feeling quite mean!"

The moon casts its glow, a spotlight so grand,
While mittens flail wildly, no one understands.
A dog in a scarf barks out a tune,
"Where's my ice cream? Why's it gone so soon?"

Icicles drip like a comical cry,
As birds try to sing, but who knows why?
They shiver and flap, their feathers askew,
"Winter's a punchline, but what can we do?"

Glow sticks at parties, all frozen in sight,
We twirl under starlight, in sheer delight.
Laughter and glitter, in chilly embrace,
In this wacky wonderland, we find our place.

Luminescence Laced with Winter's Breath

The evening is crisp, all wrapped up tight,
Bundled in layers, we're quite the sight.
A hare zooms past, a flash of white fur,
"Was that a rabbit, or a tiny blur?"

Frosty flakes decorate our jolly heads,
While we tumble around, in soft winter beds.
Slippers on our feet, we slide and we spin,
"Next year I'll skate!"—said the one with a grin.

A candy cane forest stretches so bright,
While we chase each other, in joyous delight.
A snow fort is built, but quickly attacked,
As snowballs erupt like a surprise winter act.

Stars wink down, guiding our fun,
"Who made the snow? Let's give them a run!"
With giggles and bonds growing tighter each day,
In this luminous wonder, we'll always stay.

Constellations Over Winter's Embrace

In puffy coats we trudge around,
While frozen noses make a sound.
We dance like penguins, slip and slide,
Pretending we are filled with pride.

The stars above, they twinkle bright,
We think we're funny, what a sight!
A snowball fight goes off the rails,
We laugh so hard, we tip the scales.

The air is crisp, our cheeks are red,
A snowman stands, with a plastic head.
He's got a hat that's way too big,
He's looking sharp, just like a fig!

Do the stars laugh at us, we frown?
As we trip over, fall, and clown.
In this embrace of winter's cheer,
We find the joy, we shed a tear.

Night's Chill, a Dreaming Palette

Beneath this quilt of downy white,
We prance and play, oh what delight!
Hot cocoa spills, we can't contain,
Giggling fits, we're going insane!

Snowflakes drift like tiny cats,
We chase them down with silly hats.
Our breath puffs like a train's great heave,
While Mother Nature takes her leave.

We sketch our dreams on frosty panes,
With silly shapes, in all our brains.
A penguin here, a moose over there,
With carrot noses and wild hair!

As shivering actors on this stage,
Our costumes bright, we act our age.
So here's to winter's playful jest,
In laughter's warmth, we feel the best.

Chilling Radiance Upon Earth's Canvas

The ground is crisp, a frosty sheet,
Where every step is quite a feat.
We race ahead, but then we fall,
A comic trip, we've seen it all!

With snowflakes dancing on our heads,
We build a fortress using threads.
But half the fun is in the mess,
As snowballs fly, who can guess?

Night's sparkle hits our eyes so bright,
As we pretend it's day or night.
A snowman's grin, a carrot nose,
As laughter echoes, this life glows.

So here we frolic, wild and free,
In this chill, there's glee, you see!
With every slip and every shout,
We learn what it is all about.

A Serenade of Frost and Flicker

In chilly air, we sing out loud,
While dancing like a funky crowd.
Our boots are stuck, we can't escape,
Creating art like snowy tape!

The moon peeks out, it winks, it sways,
As we giggle through the frozen haze.
Tickling toes and friendly fights,
With twinkling eyes on starry nights.

We find our joy in frosty games,
With silly shouts and funny names.
The chilly breeze plays with our hair,
While we tumble, without a care!

In laughter's light, we celebrate,
As winter's chill holds our fate.
Together we'll laugh until it's dawn,
In this whimsical, frosty lawn!

The Night's Breath in Glittering Silence

The ground is dressed in white and bright,
As snowflakes dance in the pale moonlight.
Squirrels wear their tiny boots, they prance,
While rabbits plot their midnight dance.

A frozen world, yet full of cheer,
With snowmen grinning from ear to ear.
The stars above seem to giggle down,
At the silly sight of old Frosty's crown.

Hot cocoa cups with marshmallows leap,
As everyone giggles, snuggled in sleep.
The air is crisp, but spirits so high,
Like reindeer trying to learn to fly!

So let the chill wrap you in delight,
As flurries whisper, "Stay up all night!"
With frosty faces and laughter so bright,
We'll frolic and play till morning's light.

Celestial Memories in Winter's Grasp

Stars twinkle like bling on a frosty lake,
While penguins cha-cha, for goodness' sake!
Snowball fights erupt with joyful screams,
As hot cocoa overflows, disrupting dreams.

Winter's breath has tucked the world tight,
With pillows of frost, oh what a sight!
Yet, under the moon, the moose tap their toes,
As snowflakes drift down in pirouette flows.

The night laughs with echoes of glee,
While snow-covered pups roll happily free.
They chase their tails in this wonderland,
With winter's antics—oh so unplanned!

So grab your mittens and wiggle about,
In this quirky season, there's never a doubt!
With glittering wonders, let's sing with our hearts,
For joy is the best, though snow often starts.

The Luminous Blanket of Slumbering Earth

Under the stars, a frosty delight,
Lies a world where snowflakes take flight.
They tumble and tease, like playful sprites,
In a ballet dance on chilly nights.

An igloo stands tall, with its door ajar,
Hosting a party for each little star.
They sip on moonbeams and giggle with glee,
As snowmen poke fun at a sleepy old tree.

The fox dons a scarf made of shimmering light,
While rabbits do cartwheels–what a sight!
The chill may bite, but laughter is warm,
In this winter's embrace, we weather the storm.

So let's chase the snowflakes, both big and small,
And sled down the hills as we giggle and fall.
This luminous blanket has wrapped us in cheer,
As nature wraps us in fun, my dear!

Ethereal Glimmers in the Frozen Realm

In a realm where the cool breezes laugh,
Critters all gather for a snow-filled half.
A wise old owl starts to tell a joke,
While polar bears giggle, feeling quite woke.

With fluffy white coats, they frolic with flair,
Making snow angels without a care.
The stars wink down, with a cheeky glow,
Watching the antics of our winter show.

Frosty hats are perched on igloo tops,
As wintertime music just never stops.
While penguins slide down, oh what a ride!
They might just out-dance the snowflakes beside!

So beam at the cold that makes everyone grin,
In the frosted wonder where laughter's akin.
With each twinkling moment, join in the fun,
For winter's a party—let's dance till we're done!

Winter's Palette of Shimmer and Dream

Flakes dance like tiny ballerinas,
Tickling noses in frigid arenas.
Sleds zooming by with a whoosh and a glide,
While mittens wrestle, it's a slippery ride!

Hot cocoa spills, marshmallows afloat,
As laughter erupts over frozen toes' note.
Snowmen gossip with carrots for noses,
And penguins slide down, striking funny poses.

Scarves tied up in a comical twist,
Snowball fights join the wintery tryst.
Chased by a snowdrift, a pup takes a leap,
While parents just wish for a moment of sleep!

Amidst all the whimsy, the chill in the air,
We skip and we tumble without a care.
So let's grab our hats and embrace the weird,
In this frosty realm, we laugh and we cheered!

Stars Spilling Light on Frosted Paths

Glittering beams fall like giggling sprites,
Waltzing on rooftops in twinkling tights.
While snowflakes puff like fluffy white ghosts,
They trip over each other, who they love most!

Moonlight's a painter, hilarious and bright,
Turning snowmen into creatures of fright.
One sports a top hat, the other a grin,
As squirrels chuck snowballs, where do we begin?

A snow angel flaps, so ridiculous, too,
With a laughable pose in the midnight blue.
Stars wink at the chaos, a celestial crowd,
As we tumble and giggle, so silly and loud!

In this night of wonder, with sparkle and cheer,
We dance and we prance, with no hint of fear.
So let's trip on the pathways, all sparkly and light,
As we dream up our silliness, under this night!

The Icy Embrace of Celestial Lace

Frosty patterns swirl like a merry old dance,
While we slip on the ice, what a comical chance!
Laughter erupts as we tumble and roll,
Trying desperately to hold on to control!

Gloves become sleds, oh what a delight,
As we zoom down the hill, with squeals of pure fright.
A snowball missed turns into a face-full of glee,
When the dog joins the toss, as happy as can be!

Ornaments hang on the branches above,
Twinkling like giggles, we can't help but shove.
Winter squirrels join in a mischievous plot,
With snow caps that topple, oh what a big shot!

So here in this season of laughable grace,
We'll frolic together in this chilly embrace.
With each frosty giggle and every loud cheer,
This icy wonderland brings joy, loud and clear!

Frozen Reveries in an Ethereal Night

Under the silver of a giggling mood,
The world turns whimsical, playful, and crude.
Snowflakes waltz like clowns at a fair,
While reindeer prance with style, oh so rare!

Gloves get tossed in a flurry of fun,
As popsicles melt with the glow of the sun.
Sledding down hills, we conquer with flair,
While pine trees chuckle, with stars in their hair!

With laughter that twinkles amidst frosted cheer,
We chase after joy, never showing a fear.
Pancakes flip from the griddle on high,
While syrupy snow drips as we ski by!

So sway to the music of winter's sweet laugh,
As we dance with the stars in a whimsical path.
In this frozen reverie, we twirl and we spin,
With giggles and grins, let the chaos begin!

Whispered Secrets in a Celestial Freeze

In a blanket of white where the snowmen meet,
A duck wears a scarf on its little feet.
The jolly trees giggle with hats askew,
While snowflakes chuckle, saying, "We're new!"

Bunnies in boots dance a slippery jig,
All while a squirrel tries to wiggle a twig.
With carrots for noses, they join in the fun,
As cookies and milk greet each little one.

But wait! What's this? A penguin in shades?
Strutting like royalty, through snowy cascades.
The frosty air hums with giggles and cheer,
As laughter and snowballs fly through the year.

Shimmering Pathways of Celestial Bliss

A cheeky elf slides down a hill with glee,
On a sled made of cookies, oh, can't you see?
With sprinkles for stars lighting up the night,
The jingle bell laughter brings endless delight.

Little fox with boots prances through the flakes,
Winking at owls while he twirls and quakes.
The night air is filled with sweet gingerbread,
While a grumpy old gnome just dreams of his bed.

In this wintery wonder, where funny meets freeze,
A band of bright creatures do just as they please.
With giggles and snowballs, they weep for the sun,
As twinkly-eyed raccoons join in for some fun.

A Night Cloaked in Silvery Radiance

The moon wore a hat, crooked and bright,
As it laughed at the antics of the snowy night.
With stars on their toes, the children all played,
Catching bright snowflakes that the comet had made.

A unicorn pranced with a glittery horn,
Telling tall tales of how magic was born.
While wise owls in trees spun great yarns full of glee,
The carolers chimed, "That's the best cup of tea!"

Cocoa was steaming in mugs full of cheer,
As everyone gathered, spreading joy far and near.
They danced through the snow, became jesters and
clowns,
In a world where each laugh wore a crown of soft crowns.

The Glacial Heartbeat of a Celestial Night

The snowman's hat flew off in the gust,
It landed on Fluffy, who snorted, then fussed.
With each battle cry, a sled went askew,
As zooming along, they giggled, "Woo-hoo!"

With ice-cream cone dreams and a twinkling gaze,
They fashioned a reindeer in the frosty haze.
A fairy on ice skates trips over her glow,
But laughs as she tumbles, "Oh, look at me go!"

The moon giggles softly at this merry sight,
As silly socks dance, twinkling oh-so-bright.
In a swirl of delight, the night carries on,
With humorous echoes till the break of dawn.

Winter's Glint in the Midnight Hour

When frost bites your nose and toes,
You wonder why it feels like prose.
With snowmen who wink and tease,
And sleds that glide with the greatest ease.

A cat on a branch takes a leap,
With plans for a fluffy snow heap.
He lands with a thud, oh what a sight,
As snowflakes dance in the soft moonlight.

Hot cocoa dreams with marshmallow fluff,
But spilling it all is quite the tough.
Chasing snowflakes in a dizzy spin,
You laugh, knowing winter's where to begin.

Frosty fingers turn warm and pink,
As we all gather 'round, sharing a wink.
Let's roll down the hill, no need for grace,
Just laughter and joy in this snowy place.

Cosmic Whispers on Frosty Boughs

Under twinkling lights, the trees do sway,
With critters plotting mischief on balmy hay.
Rabbits hold meetings, plotting their feats,
While the birds sing mischief from their lofty seats.

A star fell down with a gleaming plop,
In someone's mug, it made quite a slop.
Everyone laughed at the cosmic brew,
In a world where silliness felt brand new.

When the moon's grin is round and wide,
Frosty fun becomes a magical ride.
With snowballs thrown and slips on ice,
Every fall brings laughter— isn't that nice?

So grab a sled or glide on your rear,
Embrace the chill with unending cheer.
For in this winter wonder, every heart glows,
As the universe chuckles at our goofy woes.

Journeying Between Skies and Shimmer

Around the corner, who's that to see?
A penguin in boots—look out, take heed!
He wobbles and tumbles, but laughs all the way,
On this zany journey, come join the play!

Stars in the sky are hanging like balls,
While the frosty ground recalls laughter and calls.
We toss snowflakes like confetti in delight,
Who knew winter could party all night?

Sharing giggles as we skate, oh so fine,
Clumsy as moose, but hey, they shine!
With hot pie slices and quirky tales spun,
This frosty escapade surely brings fun.

So chase those stars, embrace the wild chill,
Join in the frolic, let laughter spill.
In the sparkly night, with friends all around,
Winter's peculiar magic will always be found.

Radiant Shadows of the Cold Moon

Beneath the moon, shadows do prance,
While chilly winds lead a frosty dance.
A cheeky raccoon puts on quite a show,
As the stars applaud from their heavenly row.

Mittens lost, oh, what a surprise!
A squirrel's wearing them, it's all in good guise.
With each twirl, winter seems quite absurd,
As giggles emerge, and who could be heard?

No one can walk in the deep snow's embrace,
We tumble and roll, giving nature a chase.
With laughter like echoes in the night's glimmer,
Every small slip gets a joyful shimmer.

So let's toast to the frost, where joy is the key,
Embracing the laugh of this frosty spree.
In the glow of the moon, forget all your cares,
In this season's delight, craziness shares.

Enchanted Night by the Glimmering Light

Under a sky full of twinkly lies,
A squirrel in a coat, oh what a surprise!
He dances with joy, on a branch, takes a leap,
While giggling at snowflakes that softly creep.

A penguin on skis zooms by with a cheer,
Saying, "Catch me if you can, if you dare come near!"
He slides past a rabbit wearing a hat,
Who stops for a moment, then gives him a spat.

The moon hides its face, all giggly and sly,
As the stars wink down, oh me, oh my!
A raccoon with shades rolls by on a sled,
Shouting, "Winter is wild, let's paint it red!"

Laughter erupts from the frosty scene,
As snowmen gossip, "Did you see that machine?"
With gadgets and gizmos, they all take a shot,
To build the best creature that giggles a lot!

Frosted Whispers of the Infinite

Amidst the fluff, there's a fox in a twirl,
Dressed up in a frosty, glittery swirl.
He claims he's the king of this snowy parade,
While snowflakes around him dance, unafraid.

A cat in a scarf tries to catch falling flakes,
But slips and tumbles; oh, what a mistake!
The dog laughs aloud, with a wag of his tail,
As he makes a snow angel, an epic detail.

With cocoa in hand, they gather to cheer,
For marshmallow fights that are now drawing near.
The giggles erupt in the bright chilly air,
As they trip over schmooshed marshmallows like hair!

They build a grand castle, all plump and fun,
With turrets of sugar, in bright winter runs.
But just as they crown it, the wind gives a shove,
And there goes the castle—oh, the laughs thereof!

Ethereal Glow on a Crystal Veil

In the hush of the night, upon shimmering ground,
A kitten with mittens is joyfully found.
She's looking for trouble, oh where could it be?
Perhaps in the snowballs thrown by a bee!

A moose in a tutu does an elegant prance,
While a penguin with bling tries out for a dance.
He slips and he slides, and soon takes a dive,
While critters around him hoot, "You're alive!"

With icicles hanging like jewels from a roof,
A parrot shouts happily, "Look, there's the proof!
The snow is all magic; it sparkles and glows,
Like confetti of dreams, wherever it goes!"

So gather your friends, hear the whispers of glee,
In this frosty domain, come share a hot tea.
With laughter and jokes, let's not miss a beat,
In the realm of the frost, life's nothing but sweet!

Glinting Horizons in the Midnight Numb

Beneath a chill sky, a bear finds his groove,
Wearing snowshoes, he's ready to move.
With a waddle and jiggle, he spins 'round a tree,
Saying, "This is the life, frozen frolics for me!"

An owl drinks hot cocoa, perched high on a flake,
While telling a joke about a marshmallow cake.
"The secret," he hoots, "is to add lots of fluff,
Then share it with friends, you can't have enough!"

With laughter erupting, a party unfolds,
As critters come dancing, breaking the molds.
There's a hedgehog in shades, a parsnip in boots,
Spinning round and round, delivering fruits.

At the edge of the woods, where the glimmers reside,
A snowball is launched; it's a glorious ride!
With peels of joy soaring up to the stars,
They celebrate winter, with love that is ours!

Glittering Euphoria of Winter

Frosty flakes in my hair, oh what a sight,
They dance and they twirl, what pure delight!
A snowman with carrots, a hat way too big,
He stares at my dog, who's ready to dig.

Sleds zooming by in a zigzaggy flair,
Watch out for that tree, or you'll end up in despair!
Hot cocoa spills on my nose as I sip,
Mom's cozy quilt hugs me like a warm trip.

Winter wonderland, where giggles ring loud,
In boots too big, I wobble, not feeling so proud.
But snow angels beckon, I flop on the ground,
With laughter like music, joy knows no bound.

So let's build a fort, with walls made of cheer,
A castle of dreams, no worries or fear.
Oh, winter, my friend, what silly delight,
You make every day feel perfectly bright!

Stars Weaving through Icy Air

Twinkling dots peek through a frosty haze,
They giggle at me in this wintery maze.
I chase after shadows in boots made for fun,
Close encounters with slippery ice, I'm on the run!

The moon gives a wink, what a cheeky fellow,
Gliding on snowbanks, I'm jolly and yellow.
Falling with grace, I tumble and roll,
My friends gather 'round, oh what a jesting stroll!

Bright sparkles above, I can't help but stare,
Are those stars dancing, or is it the cold air?
Snowballs in hand, oh what chaos unfolds,
As laughter erupts, winter fables are told.

With cheeks rosy red and noses a glow,
We dance in the night, let the joy overflow.
In the frosty expanse, we sing with delight,
These moments we cherish, heartwarming and bright!

A Tapestry of Crystals and Light

Glisten and gleam, the world's dressed so fine,
With frosted designs, everything's divine.
I trip on a snowdrift, land in a heap,
And dream of the sweets buried deep down in sleep.

The trees wear white coats like party attire,
"Let's boogie!" they shout, in their frosty choir.
Sipping on cider while laughter ignites,
Who knew winter parties could be such delights?

Glittery flakes swirl in a whimsical dance,
Each one a reminder of snowman's romance.
The chirps of the birds, though chilly and shy,
Are singing on branches, giving winter a try.

As icicles dangle with tips sharp and true,
I wonder if snowflakes enjoy what they do.
With a sprinkle of fun, and a twist of pure light,
This season's a blast, let's live it outright!

Winter's Lullaby in Celestial Glow

Whispers of cold in the dead of the night,
The sky overhead sprinkled with bright.
I've lost my left mitten, oh what a fuss,
But here comes a puppy, he'll help me with this!

Drifting in moonbeams, we twirl and we spin,
My hot chocolate's cooling, I take it on the chin.
The neighbors are laughing, their snowman's a sight,
With googly-eyed glasses, it's quite the delight!

We frolic like children, our breaths almost steam,
Dreaming of marshmallows, oh what a sweet dream.
The stars in the sky seem to wink and agree,
This snowy expanse plays hide-and-seek with glee.

So gather your pals, in this magic we share,
No winter blues here, only fun in the air.
With flurries of laughter and joy all around,
These chilly adventures are far more profound!

Starlit Secrets Beneath White Veils

Under blankets of the frosty stuff,
A squirrel skis, isn't that enough?
A snowman grins with carrot nose,
While giggling loudly, his belly grows.

Flakes of white fall from the sky,
As dogs leap up, asking why.
They chase their tails in a wild spree,
Wishing they could fly and see!

Children laugh, their cheeks aglow,
While hot cocoa steals the show.
With marshmallows bouncing in with glee,
It's a winter carnival, just wait and see!

The moon peeks down, a curious chap,
Watching snowball plans turn to a slap!
With each plop, a giggle erupts,
As snowmen fall, they all erupt!

Frosted Whispers and Distant Lights

Whispers of frost tickle my ear,
Is that a laugh, or just a deer?
With icicles hanging like giant blades,
Winter's jokes in crispy cascades.

Noses red as candy canes,
Sliding down hills, laughter reigns.
Wipeouts lead to roars of cheer,
Who knew winter could bring such beer?

A snowflake flutters, lands on a cat,
And somehow yes, she's gone flat!
While in the air, a dance begins,
Of jolly white elves and snow-ball spins.

And distant lights twinkle bright,
With the neighbors' ornaments, quite a sight.
Oh, baby, it's a winter bash,
But watch for trees, they tend to crash!

The Dance of Ice and Cosmic Glow

Beneath a cosmic show so wide,
A penguin twirls with mighty pride.
His dancing shoes all slick and bright,
Slide, spin, whoops! He took flight!

A comet races through the dark,
While couples skate with chick and lark.
They tumble down, what a scene,
But laughter's hearty, nothing mean!

Between the cold and frosty glee,
A rabbit hops, oh look at me!
He forgets his style; he's through the snow,
With ears flapping, putting on a show.

The stars above throw a wink or two,
As ice slips beneath, who knew!
With chirps and squeaks, the night is sound,
In a sparkling ballet, fun unbound!

Silent Serenade of Winter Nights

In a hush, the night bears white,
A raccoon sings, oh what a fright!
While snowflakes dance, they swirl and sway,
Ready to join the ancient play!

A cold breeze whispers tales of cheer,
As pine trees shrug off frozen fear.
Fuzzy mittens wave hello,
Stuck on the kids who just won't slow!

A jolly elf slips, lands with a thump,
The snowmen giggle, giving a bump.
How the reindeer twinkle, they take flight,
Chasing dreams under the pale moonlight.

So gather round, for cosmic laughs,
The winter nights, with silly halves.
With frosty jokes and stardust bright,
Let's dance until the morning light!

Whispers of Winter's Embrace

Flakes are dancing on my nose,
Making snowmen with two crows.
Laughter echoes, chilly bites,
As we prank our friends at nights.

We tripped on ice, fell on our backs,
Our only rescue? Hot cocoa snacks!
Sipping slowly, what a delight,
Giggles burst as we take flight.

The cold can be a silly chore,
Falling down, then wanting more.
With cheeks aglow and hats askew,
Winter fun is peekaboo!

In every flurry, jokes unfold,
Snowball fights are pure gold!
So here we play, no timing right,
Winter's magic feels so bright!

Celestial Crystals in the Night

Twinkling lights above my head,
I slipped and fell, and now I'm spread.
Jokes as frosty as the air,
Who needs warmth? We have our flair!

A snowman wearing grandma's hat,
Riding sleds, where's the cat?
Falling stars hide in the cold,
With silly wishes, we're so bold.

My friend once tried to dance on ice,
Landed face-first, oh so nice!
We laughed until we lost our breath,
In frozen giggles, we found our depth.

The moon grins at our winter play,
A cuddle puddle, hip-hip-hooray!
With each twinkle, chuckles reign,
Under night's charm, we'll play again!

Frost-kissed Dreams on Velvet Skies

The world gleams with a snowy glow,
Bundled up, it's quite a show!
I sent a snowball flying high,
But it bounced back—oh my, oh my!

Each flake lands with a soft touch,
Making snow angels, not too much!
Sledding down the towering hill,
Squeals of joy, and hearts that thrill.

We crafted snowmen, no two the same,
One lost its nose, what a shame!
With googly eyes and funny grins,
In winter games, we're always wins!

Frozen fingers? Not a care!
Popsicle sticks are everywhere.
Laughing as the cold bites deep,
Together in coziness, we'll keep!

Glimmering Lace of the Frozen Night

Lace of ice on every tree,
But slipping here is just for me!
I pirouette, then down I go,
It seems my dance is more for show!

Chasing flakes, we dodge like pros,
Oops, tripped on toes, oh what a pose!
Hot chocolate hugs, warming our hearts,
While outside, winter's art departs.

A caper here, a tumble there,
Every fall we seem to share.
Who knew the cold could feel so warm,
When laughter's our most charming form!

As twinkling lights begin to fade,
We find new ways to serenade.
With silly smiles and hearts so light,
We dance through all the starry night!

Echoes of Frosty Shimmers

Flakes dance lightly on my nose,
I wonder if they know it shows.
They twirl and swirl all around,
As I trip on the icy ground.

My hat flies off, I scream in glee,
Just a child, or maybe three.
Elves might laugh from up above,
Tossing snowballs with their love.

Sleds zooming down the hill so steep,
I scream for joy, can't find my feet!
The snowman winks, he's got a hat,
He's too cool, I'm just a brat.

But wait! Is that a marshmallow sprout?
It giggles loud, there's no doubt!
With every flake, the fun ignites,
In a winter world of silly sights.

Heartbeats of Light in the Winter's Grasp

The moon's a big ol' flashlight beam,
Lighting up my winter dream.
I slipped on ice, fell flat on men,
Now I waddle like a penguin.

Frosty breath makes speeches funny,
Clouds of giggles, sweet as honey.
Snowball fights bring out the cheer,
Like dodgeball, just with less fear.

I tried to make a snowman tall,
But it turned out a snowball.
With a carrot nose and smile wide,
It turned and ran—my pride has died!

Under twinkling lights we roll,
Laughter echoes in the cold.
Our hearts beat fast in chilled delight,
Winter wonder, oh what a sight!

Glacial Whispers Beneath a Sea of Stars

Stars are winking, playing tricks,
Ice cream cones have turned to bricks.
I take a scoop, it's frozen hard,
Now I'm just a winter bard.

The penguins in their tuxedos strut,
I've lost my brain, completely shut.
Snowflakes giggle, falling down,
They know they rule this frosty town.

With every slip, I crack a joke,
While sipping cocoa, I yawn and poke.
The winter chill just adds the fun,
Who knew playing in frost was a ton?

A snowball's mighty, pack it tight,
Dodge it swiftly, don't lose sight.
Under glittering frost above,
I laugh and roll, it fits like a glove.

The Choreography of Frost and Light

Ice-skating on a pea-sized lake,
A wobbly dancer—oh what a mistake!
The trees are swaying in the breeze,
They whisper secrets, down on their knees.

My socks mismatch, but who can tell?
With frosty fingers, I ring a bell.
The snowflakes cheer, they fly around,
As I tumble, playfully unbound.

My mittens are lost in the snowy drift,
They're hiding well, like a clever gift.
Two squirrels giggle from a high branch,
While I perform my clumsy dance.

In the chill, the laughter grows,
As I slip and slide with little woes.
With every star that brightens the night,
I skate and sing—what a hilarious sight!

Frozen Crystals in Celestial Clarity

Flakes dance like they've lost a bet,
Swirling down, oh what a set!
They tickle noses, make us squeal,
While we dodge them with grand zeal.

Icicles hang like crazy teeth,
Shining bright like a winter wreath.
They drip and drop in silly ways,
Turning heads in winter's craze.

Socks in boots go squish, oh joy!
With every step, we feel like a toy.
Laughter echoes, snow is a hoot,
As we slide and dance in our puffy suit.

Chasing snowmen, what a sight,
With carrot noses taking flight!
We wink at stars, full of cheer,
In this cold, frosty, funny sphere.

A Realm Where Light Meets Frost

In this place, the moon is a joke,
It casts beams that make us choke!
The frost bites hard; we shout and laugh,
In shiny coats, we take a bath.

Balloons float by, they're full of dreams,
As snowballs fly with giggling screams.
A snowman wiggles, what a sight,
His hat is way too big, so tight!

In the twinkle of the chilly night,
We march along, oh what a fright!
We trip and tumble, land on a mound,
Making angels with laughter all around.

Stars wink at us, they know our game,
As we spin and shout with wild acclaim.
This frosty land plays the best tunes,
With giggles and gleams under cartoon moons.

The Harmony of Chill and Glow

Mittens mismatched, we march along,
In this frost, we all belong.
A penguin waddles, think he's cool,
While we slip over like a fool!

Shiny paths like candy gone wild,
We chase the frost, so young and mild.
The stars giggle at our slips and flails,
As we pretend to ride on trails.

Icicles drip like a faucet's tune,
Dancing shadows beneath the moon.
We sing merry songs, at least we try,
While the soft flakes dance up to the sky.

In harmony of chill and shine,
Who knew that frost could feel divine?
With every tumble, we find new ways,
To wrap up warmth in winter's haze.

An Evening of Icy Radiance

Under twinkling lights, we strut with flair,
Wearing frosted tops, oh what a pair!
A dog in boots now pulls a sled,
While throwing snowballs at our heads!

Glitters fall like pranks from above,
A sprinkle of ice, we laugh and shove.
Spry little snowflakes on our cheeks,
In chilly bliss, our laughter peaks.

A snow path paves our way ahead,
Each step a giggle, no fear or dread.
As the moon laughs, we make a pact,
To roll and tumble, that's a fact!

Frosted giggles fill the air,
With every slip, we stop and stare.
Icy radiance wraps us tight,
As we dance home under the moonlight.

Frigid Wonders and Twinkling Skies

Frosty flakes do a little jig,
While squirrels wear hats that are far too big.
A snowman grins with a carrot nose,
And giggles come from the chilly prose.

Frosty breath forms shapes that dance,
As children toss snowballs, take a chance.
But one cheeky toss goes quite awry,
And lands on a dog who begins to cry!

The trees wear blankets, pure and white,
While birds in sweaters take to flight.
A penguin slips, does a funny twist,
Leaving snowflakes foolishly kissed!

In this frozen realm, where laughter's key,
Every flake seems to share a spree.
With giggles and slips, the night is bright,
In a world where every chill feels just right.

Shivering Elegance of Nightfall

The moon peeks out with a playful wink,
While snowmen jest and squirrels blink.
A penguin parade on a frosty spree,
Waddles along with hilarious glee.

Noses run, cheeks are red,
As laughter echoes where children tread.
Snowflakes laugh, they're light as air,
And land on hats, that's quite the fair!

In parkas that puff, all bundled tight,
Everyone rolls in frosty delight.
A snowball fight becomes a grand mess,
With laughter echoing, who feels stressed?

With frosty breath, we raise a cheer,
For each winter's folly, we hold dear.
In the elegance of this chilly land,
We twirl and laugh, hand in hand.

The Dance of Winter's Gems

Twinkling frost on the rooftop high,
While cheeky snowflakes catch the eye.
A bunny hops with a pancake hat,
Dancing like it's entirely mad!

With crystal jewels that catch a glance,
The world turns cold, yet we still prance.
"Catch me if you can!" says a winter hare,
While kids in mittens leap with flair.

A snowball launches, a surprise attack,
A snowman's nose rolls—oh, what a knack!
With laughter ringing, we take the stage,
In this winter waltz, where we engage.

As the stars twinkle and giggle too,
In this fun-filled dance, we find our crew.
Each icy flake, a scattered spark,
Lighting up the fun in the frosty dark.

A Blanket of Stillness and Brightness

Under a blanket, cozy and warm,
Silly snowflakes do their charm.
Chasing dogs, they dive and spin,
In this chaos, merriment begins.

A snow fort built with no time to spare,
As kids giggle, tossing with care.
Who knew a blizzard could wear such a grin?
With cheeks all rosy, the fun doth begin!

Chattering teeth and cheeks so round,
Echoes of laughter are all around.
With frosty noses and playful glares,
We revel in joy, shedding our cares.

In this peaceful realm, pure delight,
We dance through the gems of the chilly night.
So let us play 'til the day breaks free,
Wrapped in this blanket, just you and me!

Ethereal Dews on a Chilly Night

In the quiet, the ground wears white,
Little flakes dance, oh what a sight.
Cold air tickles as noses go red,
Fingers are frozen, but laughter's widespread.

Sipping hot cocoa, you spill on your shirt,
And giggles erupt as you wiggle in dirt.
Twirling around, with a slip and a slide,
You aim for the sofa, but crash, what a ride!

Outside the window, the chill thinks it's clever,
But in this warm room, we feel the endeavor.
With marshmallows bouncing off mugs here and there,
Each sip brings a joy beyond any compare.

So let the night glimmer, let laughter ignite,
Even frost on our cheeks can't steal the delight.
The chill may surround us, but warm hearts will gleam,
As we chuckle and giggle, living our dream.

The Celestial Waltz of Frost and Light.

Stars might twinkle, but they can't steal the show,
When snowflakes pirouette, all soft and slow.
A face full of snow when you jump in a pile,
Turns mischief to magic, and laughter to style.

Sleds flying high, with cheeks bright as cherries,
While snowmen look grumpy, dressed like old fairies.
Tobogganing down, we crash like a dream,
Rolling in white, oh, we giggle and scream.

Frosty the snowman gets a nose made of cheese,
While Fido goes chasing and slips on his knees.
We'll dance through the evening, our joy takes its flight,
In a world made of wonders, oh, what a delight!

With each flake that flutters, our spirits get light,
We play and we tumble, from dusk into night.
Forget all your worries, give them a wide berth,
This frosty más festive is all about mirth.

Whispers of Frosted Night

When moonlight wraps softly like a cozy quilt,
We giggle so loudly, it can't be distilled.
The world is so quiet, we can hear our hearts,
Bouncing and tripping as joy often starts.

Snowballs in hand, we plot out our schemes,
But laughter erupts at our 'perfect' daydreams.
You aim for my hat, but it flies through the air,
Landing on Grandma, who's unaware, unaware!

With caps and scarves on, we look quite absurd,
But the giggles we share could wake any bird.
Frosty's not friendly, he's got quite the glare,
But we can't help but laugh at his snowman despair.

As stars start to twinkle, under blankets we lie,
Counting each flake while we dream 'til we fly.
This frosted adventure, oh, what a delight,
In whispers, we giggle, through the magical night.

Celestial Dances on the White Canvas

Under a blanket of soft, glistening white,
We tumble and fumble, a true frosty sight.
With hats pulled down low, and scarves flying high,
We'll dance through the garden, and chase clouds that fly.

The trees wear their coats, a sparkling attire,
While cocoa's like magic, it's warmth we desire.
We slip on the ice, a ballet of clums,
And voices erupt with the brightest of hums.

Then suddenly still, we hear winter's call,
As snowflakes drift gently, let's try not to fall.
Evergreens giggle, their branches in sway,
We form little angels, to save us from gray.

With cheeks painted bright, we thaw all the cold,
Every mishap is turning to laughter untold.
This canvas of wonder, with joy in each glance,
Has us spinning and twirling, in a wintery dance.

Milton Keynes UK
Ingram Content Group UK Ltd.
UKHW030749121124
451094UK00013B/830

9 789916 945735